HOLMFIRTH'S SOLEMN VOICE.

A SERMON,

PREACHED IN ST. BARTHOLOMEW'S CHURCH, SALFORD,

ON SUNDAY EVENING, FEBRUARY 15TH,

IN BEHALF OF THE SUFFERERS FROM THE RECENT CALAMITOUS
VISITATION AT HOLMFIRTH.

BY THE

REV. MOSES MARGOLIOUTH, B.A.,

CURATE.

THE PROFITS TO BE APPLIED TOWARDS THE SAME CHARITABLE
OBJECT FOR WHICH THE SERMON WAS PREACHED.

LONDON:
WERTHEIM AND MACINTOSH, 24, PATERNOSTER ROW.
MANCHESTER:
SIMMS AND DINHAM, ST. ANN'S SQUARE.

POWLSON AND SON, PRINTERS, BOW-STREET, MANCHESTER.

TO THE REV. J. MOORE, B.A.,

INCUMBENT OF ST. BARTHOLOMEW'S, SALFORD,

AS WELL AS TO THE

CONGREGATION OF THAT CHURCH,

IS THIS SERMON INSCRIBED,

AS A SMALL TOKEN OF SINCERE RESPECT AND ESTEEM

FOR BOTH PASTOR AND FLOCK,

BY THE AUTHOR.

THIS Sermon is submitted to the public in deference to, and compliance with, the urgent solicitations of many who heard it delivered, and especially of those to whom it is dedicated. The Author could not conscientiously refuse compliance, since it was urged that the sale might produce a few pounds more, towards the relief-fund of the Holmfirth sufferers. This cogent reason induced the preacher to allow this humble production to encounter public opinion. The Author deems it right to add that the Sermon was delivered extempore, nevertheless there is but the slightest possible alteration, from its original; and the very few alterations are confined to verbal emendations, and not to sentiment, or argument.

The Author earnestly prays that this his humble effort may experience God's blessing, by proving a blessing to many souls.

March, 1852.

SERMON.

LUKE XIII. 1—5.

" There were present at that season some that told him of the Galileans, whose blood Pilate had mingled with their sacrifices. And Jesus answering said unto them, Suppose ye that these Galileans were sinners above all the Galileans, because they suffered such things ? I tell you, Nay: but, except ye repent, ye shall all likewise perish. Or those eighteen, upon whom the tower in Siloam fell, and slew them, think ye that they were sinners above all men that dwelt in Jerusalem ? I tell you, Nay: but, except ye repent, ye shall all likewise perish."

" COMING events cast their shadows before," is an adage which has been verified in the annals of every nation. All history, whether sacred or secular, attests to the orthodoxy of Campbell's poetic aphorism. We couple sacred and secular history together, because we consider both to be the records of the Almighty's dealings with the children of men. The former being a narrative of Jehovah's grace which He vouchsafed to fallen man ; and the latter constituting a chronicle of the Almighty's providential dispensations in the kingdoms of this earth ; and the intelligent reader of the one or the other cannot help but derive the most advantageous benefit either in the shape of encouragement, or in the character of warning.

Thus we find Israel's patriarch driven by a sore famine into the land of Egypt ; this foreshadowed, no doubt, the way by which his descendants were to be brought thither. The feuds which took place between Jacob and Esau were but shadows of the long hostile feelings which pervaded the breasts of the children of Edom against those of Israel. Joseph's vicissitudes in Egypt, first in his being employed as a confidential steward, then his being subjected to an ignominious imprisonment, and lastly, his final triumph over his enemies, — not only by quitting his dungeon, but also by being raised to great honour and wealth, —all those incidents were but presages of the great events which would be subsequently developed in the history of Zaphnath-paaneah's kinsmen. The ten plagues, which the Egyptians endured for their obstinate resistance of Jehovah's will, were but as the drops before the mighty cataract, which overwhelmed Israel's oppressors in the Red sea. We might quote many more incidents of this sort, in order to illustrate the axiom we set out with, but the few we have cited will suffice for our purpose, this evening.

We must, however, call your attention to an episode or two in secular history. Whilst the valiant Hector was loud in his boastings of Troy's invincibleness, by reason of his martial skill and early warlike training, in the midst of his impassioned harangue, he remembered that Troy was doomed to destruction. We have his feelings described by the father of Grecian bards, which has been thus paraphrased into English :—

" Yet come it will, the day decreed by fates ;
(How my heart trembles, while my tongue relates !)
The day when thou, imperial Troy, must bend,
And see thy warriors fall, thy glories end."

And about one thousand years afterwards, when that magnificent city, Carthage—the rival of Rome, the mistress of the world—was subjugated and destroyed by the skill of Scipio, that Roman general beheld all at once in the conflagration of the city of Dido, the fate of the city of Romulus ; and he is said to have given vent to a flood of tears, whilst reciting Hector's " dire presage," in reference to imperial Rome. Nor was it a mere chance effusion, for in the year 455 of our era, Scipio's presentiment was signally realized, the effects of which, Rome has never recovered. We might easily produce an array of similar, and even more striking, events, to elucidate the maxim that " coming events cast their shadows before," but time would fail us.

Besides, we have no need for any secular proof of the veracity of the theory. Does not our blessed Lord himself teach us the same important lesson, in the preceding chapter :—" And he said also to the people, When ye see a cloud rise out of the west, straightway ye say, There cometh a shower; and so it is. And when *ye see* the south wind blow, ye say, There will be heat ; and it cometh to pass. *Ye* hypocrites, ye can discern the face of the sky and of the earth ; but how is it that ye do not discern this time ? Yea, and why even of yourselves judge ye not what is right."—Luke xii. 54—57.

However to our text. The events alluded to in this laconic narrative must have taken place but a short time before the conference spoken of occurred. There were two painful calamities, which excited a vast amount of speculation and consternation. The first was brought about by the instrumentality of a wicked man, a foreigner, a Gentile, who had no right to approach the place of sacrifice; yet Pontius Pilate most sacrilegeously breaks into the sanctuary, and whilst the worshippers are in the act of immolating their various sacrifices, he puts them to death, and literally mingles their blood with their sacrifices. The second catastrophe was an immediate Providential visitation. Whilst some eighteen men were in the tower of Siloam,—doubtless watching the reservoir, or pool, of that name,—the tower fell, and buried in its ruins those individuals who were then in charge of the same. It was a fearful calamity; not only because of the great loss of life, but because of the sudden exposure of the pool of Siloam, whose waters were the main spring and stay of the inhabitants of the holy city.

The views which different parties had taken of those events were probably as diverse as their respective bias. The Pharisees, whose morning and evening delight was to contrast their self-righteousness with the apparent carelessness of their co-religionists, no doubt, looked upon the sad events as direct judgments, from the moral Governor of the universe, upon the unfortunate sufferers, for some dreadful crime. This sect must have exulted with self-complacency—as too many, alas, do in our day and generation,—over their own transcendent righteousness, till they became an offence not only to Jehovah, but also to His sober and humble followers.

Politicians, diplomatists, and philosophers might possibly have treated the disastrous catastrophes in a cold matter-of-fact sort of way. The massacre of the Galilean worshippers, whilst offering up their sacrifices, they would ascribe to the well known hostility which existed between Herod, the governor of Galilee, and Pontius Pilate, the governor of Judea; and the cruel deed, it might be said, was perpetrated as a sort of defiance, or indignity to the former.

The fall of the tower of Siloam, they would account for, by the great antiquity of the structure, by the several shocks of earthquake which were felt about that time, or to the neglect of the overseers, in repairing the foundation, which betrayed symptons of insecurity. Thus deducing the results from natural causes solely, forgetting that natural causes themselves are but the effects of the omnipotent fiat of the great First Cause,—the great I AM,—of which multitudes are "willingly ignorant of."

The sober-minded observers of the times would look seriously on those untoward events. They might not have been able to state positively what those calamities augured, but they would assuredly betake themselves to self-examination, and ask themselves,—Are we better than they who have perished? Are we prepared for such a visitation? But our blessed Lord, who knew all things, told them with unmistakeable certainty the purport of those Providential dispensations; they were intended as a warning to the impenitent, which He briefly but emphatically expressed in the portion of Scripture which we have selected as our text :—

" There were present at that season some that told him of the Galileans, whose blood Pilate had mingled with their sacrifices. And Jesus answering said unto them, Suppose ye that these Galileans were sinners above all the Galileans, because they suffered such things? I tell you, Nay: but, except ye repent, ye shall all likewise perish. Or those eighteen, upon whom the tower in Siloam fell, and slew them, think ye that they were sinners above all men that dwelt in Jerusalem? I tell you, Nay: but, except ye repent, ye shall all likewise perish."

We now desire to call your attention to the instructions, which our text contains. They may be classified under two general heads:—

I.— The dire prognostications which those calamities were to God's ancient people Israel, and,

II.—The lessons which similar calamities are intended to furnish to God's church, under the present dispensation.

May He, who hath no pleasure in the death of a sinner, but rather that he should repent and live, be in the midst of us; and may He graciously incline the hearts of those amongst us, who may have been hitherto warned in vain, to flee the wrath to come, and yield henceforth the fruit of " repentance towards God, and faith in the Lord Jesus Christ."

I.—The dire prognostications which those calamities were to God's ancient people Israel.

The prophetic import of the words of our text would appear more palpably, if we took into consideration the parable by which our Lord follows up the two matter-of-fact occurrences :—" He spake also this parable ; A certain *man* had a fig tree planted in his vineyard ; and he came and sought fruit thereon, and found none. Then said he unto the dresser of his vineyard, Behold, these three years I come seeking fruit on this fig tree, and find none : cut it down ; why cumbereth it the ground? And he answering said unto him, Lord let it alone this year also, till I shall dig about it, and dung *it :* and if it bear fruit, *well :* and if not, *then* after that thou shalt cut it down."—Luke xiii. 6—9.—We consider that parable as the most accurate exposition of our text. The nation, which is frequently represented in Scripture by the fig tree, has been long since found wanting, and deserved being cut down, that it should cumber the ground no more. The dresser of the vineyard interceded for its being let alone for another period, peradventure that by digging and dunging—figuring thereby remonstrances and chastisements—it may yet bear fruit. The massacre of the Galileans, and the fall of the tower of Siloam, were therefore instances of the digging about the fig tree mentioned in the parable.

But that which makes our blessed Lord's admonition awfully interesting, is the stress laid upon the word *likewise*, in the burden of our text. What fearful words ! Remain impenitent, and " likewise " a Roman governor, an uncovenanted

Gentile, shall sacrilegiously enter into your holy temple, and profane and defile it. Refuse to take warning, and to return to the Lord your God in this accepted time, and "likewise" strangers shall mingle your blood with your sacrifices. Harden your hearts against the messages which are now, for the last time, sent to you by me, and "ye shall all likewise perish." Your mighty towers and fortresses shall be shaken, a mighty crash shall be your death-knell, and the ruins your sepulchres. We say again, What fearful words! "Except ye repent ye shall all likewise perish." What a pang must the utterance of these ominous syllables have been to the meek and lowly Jesus, who so loved the world as to lay down his life for the children of men. Yes! He who was altogether lovely, and who always spoke so lovingly, how painful must have been his experience when the burden of His remonstrance was, "Ye shall all likewise perish." And how should those ominous syllables have echoed and re-echoed in the ears of the daughter of Zion, and the inhabitants of Jerusalem! How should that fearful prophecy have aroused them to repentance! But, alas, the things which belonged to their peace were hid from them.

But you may be wishful to know whether this dreadful "likewise" has ever received any fulfilment? Yes, to the letter! Soon after Cumanus was appointed procurator, the Roman soldiery were encouraged to outrage the sanctity of the temple; and because the people resisted the profane procedure of that procurator and his army, the blood of twenty thousand Israelites was mingled with the blood of their sacrifices. Three thousand six hundred perished in the same manner, under the procuratorship of Florus, the protegé of the brutal Nero. Fearful in length, and frightful in amount, is the account of the massacres which took place, after the crucifixion of the Saviour of the world by the people to whom He came, and who rejected Him. The harrowing details of that period, as described by the co-temporary Josephus, sufficiently prove that the fatal prophecy "likewise" received its fulfilment, in the strictest sense of the word.

Jewish tradition is not backward in bearing witness to the accurate fulfilment of the tremendous prophecy of our text. "Rabbi Chiya bar Abin said that Rabbi Joshua ben Korcha said,—'an aged individual of the men of Jerusalem told me, that when the enemy entered into the temple, he found the blood of Zechariah in a restless and boiling condition; he asked what blood it was? the Jews answered, that of sacrifices which had been spilt. He then ordered blood [of animals] to be brought, but there was no comparison; he then said to the Jews, if you tell me, well and good, but if not, I shall comb your flesh with iron combs. They replied, Shall it be told that we had a prophet, who expostulated with us in the name of heaven, and that we rose against him, and murdered him, and behold now, many are the years that his blood is thus restless. He said to them, I shall conciliate him. He then brought the higher house of the Sanhedrim and the lower house of the Sanhedrim, and slaughtered them over the blood, but it was not appeased. He then slaughtered all the young men and young women, over the blood, but it was still restless; he then brought the school children, and slaughtered them over the blood, and yet there was no change. He then said, Oh Zechariah, Zechariah, I have already slain the best amongst them; if it please thee, I will destroy *all* of them. As he said this, the blood was at rest.'"* Poor Jews, according to your own showing, Jesus was a true prophet.

" Except ye repent, ye shall all likewise perish." Their blood was spilt till the valleys presented large scarlet lakes, for " likewise " was the burden of Him who is untainted in His holiness, unbending in His justice, and unchanging in His truth. Tower after tower fell and buried their thousands and

---

* This tradition is to be found in Talmud, Treatise GUITIN, and it also occurs, with some modification, in Josephon ben Gorion; and it is formed into a melancholy Hebrew elegy, which the Jews, throughout the dispersion, recite on the anniversary of the destruction of the temple by Titus.

tens of thousands, for not one jot or tittle can fall to the ground, of what Jesus foretold, and He predicted that " except ye repent, ye shall all likewise perish." We might easily analyse the whole dread story of the conflicts and conquests of Jerusalem, and prove to you, step by step, the fulfilment of the fatal "likewise;" but what we have advanced is perfectly sufficient for our purpose.

To judge of the sad, yet affectionate, feelings of our Saviour, whilst He pronounced the doom of His beloved people and city, we must listen to His tender and heart-rending moanings over them, which is to be found in the thirty-fourth verse of this chapter,—" O Jerusalem, Jerusalem, which killest the prophets, and stonest them that are sent unto thee; how often would I have gathered thy children together, as a hen doth gather her brood under her wings, and ye would not!" How often would I have gathered thy children together! I would have gathered you together, when Pompey besieged Jerusalem, and would have spared the vast effusion of your blood, if ye had but repented; but ye would not. I would have gathered you together, when the Idumean began to trample upon you, if ye had but repented; but ye would not. I would have gathered you together, when the wise men arrived from the east, to enquire after the place of my incarnation. I would have gathered you together, when Herod put to death your innocent infants, at

Bethlehem, if ye had but repented;—but ye would not. And the verdict has been therefore most irrevocable, at the close of this chapter:—"Behold, your house is left unto you desolate : and verily I say unto you, Ye shall not see me, until the time come when ye shall say, Blessed is he that cometh in the name of the Lord."

II.—The lessons which similar calamities are intended to furnish to the Church of God, during this present dispensation.

The history of the Jewish nation is not, as some suppose, obsolete and unimportant, in the present dispensation. Nothing but lamentable ignorance of the Scriptures of truth could suggest such an idea. The fact is, the history of Israel, is—using the words of the royal and inspired bard—a parable for the instruction of all nations. The Psalm which we read this evening,* begins thus :—" Give ear, O my people, to my law: incline your ears to the words of my mouth. I will open my mouth in a parable : I will utter dark sayings of old : which we have heard and known, and our fathers have told us. We will not hide them from their children, showing to the generation to come the praises of the Lord, and His strength, and His wonderful works that He hath done." The Psalmist then proceeds with a minute and succinct account of the

* February 15.

events which befel the people of Israel, and yet David calls the narrative " a parable." What does this teach us, but the same truth which the great Apostle of the Gentiles was solicitous to impress upon an early Gentile Christian Church, when he was treating of the history of God's ancient people. He says, " Now all these things happened unto them for ensamples : and they are written for our admonition, upon whom the ends of the world are come."

Our text, therefore, is of the greatest possible importance to us, especially at the present moment, when the effects of a most disastrous catastrophe, just occurred, cry aloud in our ears. Our text teaches *us*, therefore, in the first place, that those who suffer, are not always the most guilty. For it is Jesus himself who asked the question, "Suppose ye that these Galileans were sinners above all the Galileans, because they suffered such things ? * * * Or those eighteen upon whom the tower in Siloam fell, and slew them, think ye that they were sinners above all men that dwelt in Jerusalem ?" To both of which queries, the Omniscient interrogator gives the same unequivocal answer, " I tell you NAY." But the same Jesus teaches us, in the second place, that such calamities are sent as solemn national warnings, and whenever they take place, the professing follower of God, is to be up and doing; for we are told by the same unerring and truthful lips, "except ye repent, ye shall ALL LIKEWISE perish." Such frighful calamities should make us tremble, not only for our personal security, but for our national safety.

We have no sympathy with those who are wise over much, and affect to be too philosophical to take cognizance of such occurences, as direct messages from the invisible world. No, we willingly give up such wisdom; our wisdom is rudimental, whereby we would gladly abide. For a man after God's own heart, left us on record, that "the fear of the Lord is the beginning of wisdom; a good understanding have all they that do His commandments." We strive, therefore, to be simple, unsophisticated believers in our blessed Saviour's declarations and doctrines.

We have no hesitation in saying, not only before you, but before the whole of British Christendom, that we consider the fatal and dire catastrophe which has just occurred at Holmfirth, as a voice from heaven to the British nation, and, therefore, to every British family; ay, and to every British individual, saying, "Except ye repent, ye shall *all likewise* perish." Yes, a warning to the whole nation! Providential dispensations are no more local; the facilities of locomotion, and that wonderful agency, the electric telegraph, render every occurrence trumpet-tongued, throughout the length and breadth of this mighty kingdom. In a few hours after its occurrence, was the fearful event at Holmfirth published in every corner of the country; and every individual whose breast throbbed with sympathy for the afflicted, must have experienced an aching of heart, for the destitute, the fatherless, and widows, which the inundating waters of that mighty reservoir were the means of making. But is this all? Is the sympathy which a naturally kind heart manifests, the only thing which this catastrophe was intended to elicit? Was it sent for no other purpose than to afford an opportunity to those who have heaped up riches for *themselves*, against the day of wrath, to display a trifle of mock generosity, from their vast abundance towards the homeless, naked, and hungry, and thus gratify a pharisaical disposition? No, no! As ambassadors for Christ, we are bound to speak, not only in His name, but to preach also from His Word; and we therefore point to Holmfirth, and say to you, in the words of our Lord, "Suppose ye that these Galileans were sinners above all the Galileans, because they suffered such things? I tell you, Nay: but, except ye repent, ye shall all likewise perish."

Brethren, this is a seasonable time to lift up *our* voices and cry aloud, "Judge yourselves, that ye be not judged of the Lord." Enter into a rigid and searching examination of your hearts. Ascertain whether it is wholly given to the Lord your God, or whether you are Christians in name only, like the Scribes, Pharisees, and Sadducees, in the days of our Lord, who were Jews outwardly, but inwardly a "generation of vipers." I entreat you, dearly beloved, not to be satisfied with your condition, if you only resemble whited sepulchres. Be ye assured, that just as apostate Judaism was judged at the first coming of our Saviour, so shall apostate Christendom be judged at the second coming of the Judge of the whole earth; and to this agree the words of the Prophets. And the same sacred oracles assure us that, just as dire calamities and frightful prodigies preceded the utter dismemberment and severe judgment of Israel, likewise shall it come to pass before Christendom had filled up the measure of her sins. Happy would it have been for Israel if they had given heed to the exhortation of our Lord, and took warning by the foreboding calamities, and repented; but they would not. Wars, and rumours of wars, were constantly before them; but they repented not. Pilate mingled their blood with their sacrifices; but they repented not. The tower of Siloam—of peace—fell, and destroyed many a man; and thus, also, was the pool of Siloam lost to the nation; but they repented not. Terrific omens and prodigies affrighted them;* but

---

* Many were the ominous signs which preceded the final

D

they repented not. Time would fail me, were I to enumerate all the solemn warnings sent to " my

destruction of the holy city and temple. Josephus informs us that a star, resembling a sword, stood over the city, and a comet remained a whole year in the sky. The gates of brass, on the east of the inner court of the temple, which were closed in the evening, with difficulty, by not less than twenty men, opened suddenly of themselves, in the sixth hour of the night. Before the destruction of the city, chariots and armed troops were seen in the clouds, stretching far over the city, and surrounding it. At the feast of tabernacles the priests heard at night, in the temple, a sound of many voices, crying, " Let us go hence." But a more remarkable presage was manifested through a peasant, named Joshua, who came to Jerusalem to the feast of tabernacles, four years before the breaking out of the war, and went day and night through the streets of the city, crying out with a loud voice, " Woe to Jerusalem, the temple, and the whole people !" He was brought before Albinus, the governor, who ordered him to be scourged to the bone : no groan, however, escaped his lips, but at every stroke the awful cry was, " Woe, woe to Jerusalem." To every question as to who he was, whence he came, and why he so cried out, he answered nothing but " Woe, woe to Jerusalem ;" so that the governor at length released him as a lunatic. Till the commencement of the war he associated with no one, nor was he ever seen to speak to any one ; but day by day he cried, as though it had been his prayer, " Woe to Jerusalem." He cursed not them that smote him, nor thanked them that gave him food ; his only answer to every one was the fatal prophecy. So did he daily, but most loudly at the feasts, for seven years and five months, without becoming either hoarse or tired, till he saw the fulfilment of the prophetic words in the siege of the city. As he was, however, one day running about the city walls, with the cry, " Woe to the city, to the people, and brethren, my kinsmen according to the flesh; for whom I have great heaviness, and continual sorrow of heart."

But, dear brethren, can we be blind or deaf to the many warnings which we have seen and heard? Take a retrospective view of the last ten years; count up the ships you have lost by sea, with thousands of your countrymen; enumerate your national losses by land, by the devouring and devastating element, fire, in one shape or another; reckon up the amount of the fatal accidents that befel your co-patriots by railways and balloons. Transfer yourselves for a moment to some of your colonies, and behold the state of things there, I need not particularize, you know to what I refer. Now come back nearer home, and contemplate the disastrous catastrophe of Holmfirth, which is but of yesterday, as it were, and judge for yourselves. I speak as unto wise and sober men, and ask you whether it is not high time to be aroused from the lethargy of indifference and callousness; whether the expression, " how often would I have gathered you together, but you would not," may not be ultimately as applicable to the sons of Britain, as it was once to the children of Judea. We will not, we dare not, speak with the same positive certainty of the import

the temple," he added suddenly, " Woe also to me!" and at the same moment, being struck by a missile from the besiegers, he gave up the ghost.

of the fatal events, which befal this country, as our Lord spoke of those which happened unto Israel; but we may safely adopt, in the first place, the words of an Israelite when preaching to, and reasoning with, Gentiles :—" Moreover, brethren, I would not that ye should be ignorant, how that all our fathers were under the cloud, and all passed through the sea; and were all baptized unto Moses in the cloud and in the sea; and did all eat the same spiritual meat; and did all drink the same spiritual drink : for they drank of that spiritual Rock which followed them : and that Rock was Christ. But with many of them God was not well pleased : for they were overthrown in the wilderness. Now these things were our examples, to the intent we should not lust after evil things, as they also lusted. Neither be ye idolators, as were some of them; as it is written, The people sat down to eat and drink, and rose up to play. Neither let us commit fornication, as some of them committed, and fell in one day three and twenty thousand. Neither let us tempt Christ, as some of them also tempted, and were destroyed of serpents. Neither murmur ye as some of them also murmured, and were destroyed of the destroyer. Now all these things happened unto them for ensamples : and they are written for our admonition, upon whom the ends of the world are come. Wherefore let him that thinketh he standeth take heed lest he fall."

And having such a precedent, we may even boldly adopt the statement of Him, who knew all things, and say, " Suppose ye that they were sinners above all others, because they suffered such things? I tell you, Nay : but, except ye repent, ye shall all likewise perish." Some may feel disposed to smile at such interpretations of such events, but we feel nothing abashed or daunted, either in the presence of ignorant smiles, or at the sneers which professors of philosophy, falsely so called, may be disposed to indulge in. We are believers in the doctrines of this sacred Volume, and bear a commission from the KING of Kings, and LORD of Lords, who " turneth wise men backward, and maketh their knowledge foolish."* Or as St. Paul has it, " Hath not God made foolish the wisdom of this world !"†

It is idle to maintain that any trustees are the sole cause of the lamentable catastrophe: we believe in a FIRST CAUSE, of whom, and through whom, and to whom are all things, who is God over all blessed for ever. To which agree the words of the Psalmist: " Come, behold the works of the Lord, what desolations He hath made in the earth. He maketh wars to cease unto the end of the earth; He breaketh the bow, and cutteth the spear in sunder; He burneth the chariot in the fire." Jehovah then appears, and addresses the wise in their own conceit,

* Isaiah xliv. 25.   † 1 Cor. i. 20.

saying, "Stand still, and know that I am God."

We reiterate our belief, therefore, that the recent catastrophe of Holmfirth is a warning voice to the nation from the invisible world, saying, "Except ye repent, ye shall all likewise perish." God is long suffering, and of tender mercies; many years may elapse before the threatening is put into execution, as it was in the case of the Israelites, but sooner or later it must be verified, "except ye repent." Oh! may the exhortation, "except ye repent," sink deeply into all our hearts, so that to "obtain repentance" may be the chief aim of the remainder of our lives. Oh! what a call is not this catastrophe to self-examination!

But, methinks, I hear some one say, "Tell us how to begin this new career which you so emphatically recommend."

Begin it according to the counsel which Daniel gave to Nebuchadnezzar:—"Wherefore, O King, let my counsel be acceptable unto thee, and break off thy sins by righteousness, and thine iniquities by showing mercy to the poor: if it may be a lengthening of thy tranquility." It is an important fact that both in the Old and New Testaments, "*showing mercy to the poor*," is considered as infallible fruits of righteousness. The verdict which is to be given at the last great assize, is to be in accordance with the performance of the duty alluded to:—"When the Son of Man shall come in His glory, and all the holy angels with Him, then shall He sit upon the throne of His glory: and before Him shall be gathered all nations: and He shall separate them one from another, as a shepherd divideth his sheep from the goats: and He shall set the sheep on His right hand, but the goats on the left. Then shall the King say unto them on His right hand, Come, ye blessed of my Father, inherit the kingdom prepared for you from the foundation of the world: for I was an hungred, and ye gave Me meat: I was thirsty, and ye gave Me drink: I was a stranger, and ye took Me in: naked, and ye clothed Me: I was sick, and ye visited me: I was in prison, and ye came unto Me." It is an instructive picture, and the transcendent beauty of it consists in the feature of identity between Christ and the poor, as the subsequent verses plainly prove.

Dearly beloved, ye cannot begin better your career of repentance than by "showing mercy to those poor" who became so from this catastrophe. I beseech you to show them pity for your own sakes. Indeed, I am disposed to believe that this trial has already begun to work the peaceable fruits of righteousness amongst us. It is to an individual of this congregation, that this appeal owes its origin. Let us, therefore, come behind with no one, but let us all unite together in contributing something towards this loudly called for charity; and let us do it in the spirit of David, who spoke thus :—" Thine, O Lord, is the greatness, and the power, and the glory, and the victory, and the majesty : for all that is in the heaven and in the earth is Thine; Thine is the kingdom, O Lord, and Thou art exalted as head above all. Both riches and honour come of Thee, and Thou reignest over all ; and in Thine hand is power and might ; and in Thine hand it is to make great, and to give strength unto all. Now therefore, our God, we thank Thee, and praise Thy glorious name. But who am I, and what is my people, that we should be able to offer so willingly after this sort ? for all things come of Thee, and of Thine own have we given Thee." Let us never forget that we are but stewards of the silver and gold of which we seem the possessors. Let us therefore do our duty in the present instance : let each of us give something towards the relief of the distressed of Holmfirth ; let each of us give according to our ability; and let each of us give cheerfully, not grudgingly, or as of necessity. Let us take a lesson from the poor Negro Christians, and let us go and do likewise.*

Now to God the Father, &c., &c.

---

* Such were the three first *resolutions*, of a small band of poor Negro Christians, in Africa, who formed themselves into an Auxiliary Association to the noble Church Missionary Society.

In a few days will be published by the same Author.

GENUINE FREEMASONRY,

INDISSOLUBLY CONNECTED WITH REVELATION:

A LECTURE DELIVERED IN THE WORTHY AND WORSHIPFUL LODGE OF VIRTUE (177), MANCHESTER.

CONTENTS.

The excellencies of Freemasonry irresistibly commendable to the intelligent, even to such as are uninitiated.—Masonry not only "a beautiful system of morality," but also a peculiar system of revealed religion, "veiled in allegory and illustrated by symbols."—The supposed union of *speculative* and *operative* Masonry, the source of fruitful misconceptions amongst many brethren.—The principle of Masonry traceable to the dawn of revelation.—Its mysteries were communicated by degrees, to "few and far between."—The rise and fall of Masonry synchronise with the health and decline of the Church of God.—Frequent allusions to the science, by the prophets.—Its preservation amongst the Israelites in Babylon.—Pythagoras met Daniel at Babylon.—The extraordinary development of the mysteries, when the great Architect of the Universe was manifested in the flesh.—The tests peculiarly beautiful.—Their literal and real meanings.—The allegory and symbol of the third degree august and sublime.—The murderous conspiracy of Caiaphas, Herod, and Pontius Pilate graphically pourtrayed.—Repeated allusions to our mysteries by the Apostles.—By the early Hebrew divines.—Preservation of Freemasonry, to this day, by the instrumentality of Orthodox Christians.—The necessity that the practice of the Brethren should correspond with the precepts of Freemasonry.

READY FOR THE PRESS.

TO BE DEDICATED, BY PERMISSION,

TO THE RIGHT REV. THE LORD BISHOP OF MANCHESTER.

תורה נביאים וכתובים

THE HEBREW OLD TESTAMENT,

WITH

CRITICAL, PHILOLOGICAL, HISTORICAL, POLEMICAL, AND EXPOSITARY ENGLISH COMMENTS;

THE PRINCIPAL PORTIONS OF WHICH ARE ORIGINAL.

IN THREE VOLUMES,

(650 pp. IN EACH VOLUME.)

The Author humbly trusts that, with the blessing of God, the work which he has set before himself to accomplish, will not only prove useful to the advanced Theological Student, but also an important auxiliary to the Bible reader in general, who may be altogether unacquainted with the sacred tongue.

To make the Work more acceptable, a new fount of Hebrew type will be cast for the purpose.

Price to Subscribers, Three Guineas— One Guinea to be paid in advance, to defray current expenses—to Non-subscribers, Four Guineas.

The Work will be proceeded with as soon as an adequate number of Subscribers is secured to warrant the expenses of the press.

WORKS BY THE SAME AUTHOR.

I. The HISTORY of the JEWS in GREAT BRITAIN. In three vols., post 8vo.—RICHARD BENTLEY.

"The minute and patient research here bestowed on the history of the Jews in England, has brought to light a mass of curious information, of which few have any idea. The work is one of real value, in more ways than one; especially as containing fragments of history almost inaccessible."—*Presbyterian Review.*

"These volumes are invested with great historical value and importance."—*Caledonian Mercury.*

"A very complete and interesting history of the Jews in England. The author writes with candour and impartiality."—*Weekly Chronicle.*

II. A PILGRIMAGE to the LAND of MY FATHERS. Two vols. 8vo. With numerous Illustrations.—RICHARD BENTLEY.

"The Letters which he (Mr. M. M.) addressed to me were replete with interesting information. The friends to whom I communicated them, read them with as much pleasure as I had done; and I believe him to be not only singularly qualified to draw out and discover what is curious in the countries that he visited, but likewise very happy in his manner of describing them."—*The Worshipful and Rev. Chancellor Raikes.*

"So ends our review of a work which has entertained us with a variety of topics, treated in an original way."—*Literary Gazette.*

"The work abounds in curious details concerning the condition and opinions of the Jewish populations of the various countries in Europe, Asia, and Africa, which the author visited. Some of the disclosures, too, are as astounding and romantic as anything in Mr. Disraeli's fictions, and with the additional advantage of being not inventions but truths........ Of the more learned portion of the work, its critical and antiquarian discussions, we despair of giving an adequate account. They embrace a great variety of subjects, and are highly creditable to the author's learning and ability."—*Daily News.*

"He appears to be thoroughly conversant with Hebrew literature, and his notices of its poetry, and occasional specimens of Hebrew music, are curious."—*Examiner.*

"Mr. Margoliouth is a man evidently of a practical turn of mind........ We can safely recommend his volumes not only to those who read for amusement, but those who read for instruction."—*Weekly News.*

"As a traveller, he has given to the world some new information, for he had peculiar opportunities of access to localities and persons and domestic scenes, which only one who spoke the language of the Jews, and was acquainted with their customs and habits, could have penetrated. His account of the Jews of Paris is as interesting as any part of the narrative, and strange to say, it is a topic undescribed even by the anatomisers of Parisian society."—*The Critic.*

"It is replete with information as varied as it is valuable, as curious as it is attractive."—*Britannia.*

III. An EXPOSITION of the FIFTY-THIRD CHAPTER of ISAIAH. One vol. 8vo.—WERTHEIM AND MACINTOSH.

Extract from a Letter to the Author, by the late Bishop of Kildare:—

"My dear Margoliouth,—I return you the two last of a series of sermons, which it would be unjust to withhold from the public at large," &c.

"Able, learned, and most profitable throughout. To the scholar it will be most interesting."—*Presbyterian Review.*

"The author's whole aim is to demonstrate its vital importance, for which purpose he takes it verse by verse, and comments upon each expression critically, historically, polemically, and practically........ We feel that we are quite safe in commending these Lectures to the attentive perusal of all who are interested in this most wonderful prophecy."—*English Review.*

IV. The FUNDAMENTAL PRINCIPLES of MODERN JUDAISM INVESTIGATED. One vol. 8vo.—WERTHEIM AND MACINTOSH.

"Your luminous book, which suggests a most valuable alteration in the course hitherto pursued by young students in theology, has not yet been a sufficient time before the public to excite attention......... Your 'Investigation of Modern Judaism' I have read several times throughout with great attention. That work, with Mr. Chancellor Raike's preface, and your short memoir, form a compendium of much value to theological students, because it brings together one whole subject of Talmudical learning which they have had to collect from various authors."—*Extracts from Letters from the Right Rev. Charles Lindsay, D.D., late Lord Bishop of Kildare.*

V. ISRAEL'S ORDINANCES EXAMINED. 8vo. WERTHEIM AND MACINTOSH.

"We do not know of any one whose reply we should look for with more interest than Mr. Margoliouth's; and on a perusal of his little pamphlet, we have found it just as happy in its spirit as it is conclusive in its arguments."—*Christian Examiner.*

Powlson and Son, Printers, Bow-street, John Dalton-street, Manchester.

www.ingramcontent.com/pod-product-compliance
Lightning Source LLC
Chambersburg PA
CBHW081308040426
42452CB00014B/2698